To all our customers, near & far…

Good and bad

(You know who you are!)

This book would not have been possible without you!

***

I would also like to dedicate this book to my good friends and co-workers (you also know who you are!!)

It has been a blast working with you!

I will remember you always.

CHAPTERS

If this book had chapters, they would be entitled the following (actually, some of them are really chapters in the book):

Chapter 1: Epic Employees (A real chapter)

Chapter 2: Krazy Kustomers (Biggest chapter by far)

Chapter 3: Menu Mispronunciations or "I'll have the Veggie-Wedgie" (Another real chapter).

Chapter 4: Pastrami Faux Pas (Can that be heated?)

Chapter 5: Things we get asked repeatedly. I think I will make this a chapter.

Chapter 6: Italian Flub ("Oops. I meant to order something else.")

Ok, I'm probably not going to make the rest of these chapters, so I'm going to stop pretending I am...

Six hundred Grain (It can't get any healthier)

Hamming it Up (Behind the scenes)

Salami for your troubles (The customer is always right)

Capicolla Outbreak (It's more than just a deli meat)

Provo -leave us a- lone (We close at 2:00)

AvacaNO (Get your uppity food elsewhere)

Weevil Get You (What they don't know won't hurt them)

CONDIMENTS!!!!!! (A few helping verbs, PLEASE)

It's just not kosher (people steal stuff) This will get a brief mention.

So, chapters or no chapters, follow along and take a peek at what goes on behind the scenes of a REAL Deli someplace in New England...

Chapter 1 EPIC EMPLOYEES

Just to set the scene, I must start by saying that the employees in our fine establishment are, literally, awesome. Starting out at the top, the Owner is innovative, kind, and generous. He is a visionary, and wonderful to work for. The Manager is amazing, and runs the place with great love and care for all of us. We have been very fortunate that most of our employees are great, responsible people. We have been there for a long, long time. We truly care about each other, are supportive of each other, and keep each other laughing.

Consider the following exchange...

Customer: "Do you have table service?"

One of our witty employees: "No table service...we don't even clean the tables!"

And this embarrassing moment...

While standing in line to order, there was a screaming kid somewhere that we could hear but not see. He/she kept yelling "Mommy...Mommy!" over and over. Our exasperated employee finally yelled out, "Will somebody please answer that kid?!?" As it turned out, their parent was standing right in front of the employee, and they finally did answer their kid.

So we are human, funny, and embarrassing. But we do our best! There have been the rare few, temporary employees, however, that were memorably awful...

There was the woman employee who told me on my first day that she would be working at this particular deli for the rest of her life. She was about 31 at the time. She is no longer working there; however, I am.

She also taught me how to run the register. She specifically said, "When a customer pays with a credit card, tell them to have a nice day. That way they will trust you." She added, "You don't have to tell the cash customers to have a nice day!"

One memorable employee of only one day, spilled something on her shoe, wiped it off with one of the counter rags, and was let go on the spot...pun not intended!

One of our employees needed to be "let go" due to laziness and other less than excellent work ethic, such as spending 20 minutes at a time in the bathroom several times a day and putting the unwelcome moves on other employees. When he came in to work one day, the manager told him she regretfully had to terminate his employment. He became quite angry and sputtered at all the stunned employees listening to this incident, "I know about you...all of you...you are always ON TIME!" (I guess lateness was his other flaw, but it hadn't been mentioned).

Other employees no longer with us (as in they have moved on to other places of employment):

The blond girl who had a tendency to lunge suddenly across the counter to feel the material of many a shocked customer's shirt. She also had a tendency to throw her garbage away quite carelessly all day, so by the end of the day the wall above the trash can was covered with pieces of vegetables and globs of mayo. Still another unattractive trait of hers was her penchant for throwing down the cutting knives with wild abandon ("HEY..watch it, that's my hand, there!!")

Another employee, while washing the dishes, would slam them around as loudly as possible when angry, which was quite often. The other employees would cringe and feel terrified during these episodes.

But that was in the distant past. Most of our recent and present employees have lasted for many years, and are still our good friends. We would welcome them back any time, either to work or to visit.

All in all, we are a great group of friends who care about ourselves and the nice customers who come into our deli. We even try to care about the not-so-nice ones!

Chapter 2: KRAZY KUSTOMERS, We got 'em (For some reason, this is the longest chapter in the book).

One thing you learn when you work in the food business, or any customer service business, for that matter, is that "People are People wherever you go." Another one is (as my father always says) "It takes all kinds to make a world."

And that is what makes deli life interesting; the many characters that come to 'visit' us in the deli. And I do mean characters. We could make a play (skit? comedy act?) out of them. So, to that end, here is a compilation of comments and questions from some of our most memorable patrons. The contents herein are entirely true.

The front counter in our deli has many LARGE signs to instruct customers on where to order, where to pay, and what is on the menu. The large 6 foot by 4 foot menu is the first thing they can't find. Then the customers stand in front of the large red and white "ORDER HERE" sign and ask where to order. Then they don't see the gargantuan cash register right next to the counter. And so on...sigh

MORE SILLY QUESTIONS:

Customer: "When does your Day-Old-Bread become Day-Old-Bread???"

***

Customer: "Where is the Restroom?"

Us: "Right under that gargantuan RESTROOM HERE sign with the arrow pointing at the restroom door!"

Customer: "Do you have any beverages?"

Us: "Yes, about 40 different ones in those 2 large coolers right beside you!" or "No, we are the only restaurant on earth that only serves food and makes you go thirsty while eating it."

Us, to Customer: "Would you like a bag?"

Customer: "Blonde or Brunette?!"

***

PLEASE DON'T HELP US GET TIPS!

We had a talkative woman customer who noticed that our "Tip Basket" didn't have very much money in it.

She began to lament that people were just not generous enough and what a shame that was for us. She gave us a $20 tip and promised to make us a new and better sign, which she was convinced was our problem. She said she was an artist and she would make us a GREAT sign for our tip basket.

A few weeks later she did return with a new, originally designed sign for our tip basket. It was approximately one and a half feet long, and in childish scrawl she had created a sign which said "DESPERATE" and "SAVE the DELI". My kindergarten daughter could have done better. We hid the sign and hoped she wouldn't notice. She didn't.

UPDATE: The woman returned again a year later and began coming in every day for the summer season. She was apparently unconcerned this time about our empty basket, as she never once left a tip. She DID however, mumble many times to herself about how we were "killing" her (the prices, I presume?) She also announced, to no one in particular, that she had a brain tumor. After a while, we began to believe her.

Similarly, a woman yelled angrily while signing her credit card slip, "ARE WE SUPPOSED TO TIP YOU!?" Me, meekly, "No."

Customer, wanting us to heat up take-out food, which we do not do: "If I ask you real nice, will you heat up this chicken pot pie?"

Us: "No, but if I tell you 'no' real nice, will you still leave us a tip???"

NO, YOU CANNOT HAVE FREE FOOD

There is the man who comes up to the register and whispers "Can I have some extra (meaning free) chips?!" (WINK, Wink!)

Our response: "If we give you extra free chips then EVERYONE will want them (WINK, WINK!!!!)

Woman who is RAVING about the place. "I came 3,000 miles for a sandwich and chips!!!! (she ordered turkey and bread, dry). "I've been DREAMING about the chips for a week straight!!!!" Then she is asked to pay $8.35 for her lunch. She balks: "ARE YOU SERIOUS?!?!?!?!?!?"

Another exchange with a raving uh...customer went as follows...

Me: "Would you like chips with your sandwich?"

Customer gushes: "OH GOD!!!!! Yes!!!!!!!!!!!!!! I just drove 5 hours for these chips!!!!!!!!!!!!" (Ok, calm down. They are just potatoes fried in oil.)

There was once a man who sprayed Windex all over his hands and rubbed them together to "clean" them. Hmmm..

Another customer came out of our bathroom with our brand new bottle of Febreeze sticking out of his pocket? We were so stunned, we all just looked at him. Probably told him to have a nice day!

Speaking of stealing, we have had our bathroom mirror stolen (which had been attached to the wall!) And also many bottles of expensive lotion (which were not attached). And there's our refill situation...

We do not offer free refills on fountain soda. It is $1.00 for a refill. Most people do not ask, and they just assume they are free. Some people take water cups and fill them with soda...without paying. The biggest culprits were the couple I liked to refer to as "The Iced Tea Thieves." These people were regulars, and they were told repeatedly that there are no free refills, so they knew the ropes. But they continued to ignore this rule and every time they came in they took free refills. I kept moving the iced tea dispenser until finally it was behind the counter were they could not go.

Many customers fight with each other over who's going to pay the bill. They throw their credit cards at the cashier and she is asked to decide who is paying. The person who is being bought a free lunch is not grateful to be paid for. In fact, they get ANGRY at each other and shake their heads disgustedly. Others of them will whisper to the cashier that they are paying for themselves as well as the next 3 people. But they say, "Don't tell them, just use my card." However, after the bill is paid, the first customer tells them anyway, and basks in their own generosity.

DECISION, DECISIONS...

Many customers are completely indecisive when it comes to ordering, or selecting the type of bread for their sandwich. Some of them don't even try.

Server: "What kind of bread would you like?"

Customer, shrugging, "I don't know." Impasse.

One man thought he knew what he wanted. He ordered a ham sandwich with honey- mustard. When the employee began making his sandwich, he began shouting, "WHOA!! WHOA!!!! Is that honey-mustard??!?!"

"Yes," she answered. "Didn't you ask for honey-mustard?"

Man: "Yes," he answered. "But I changed my mind!!"

Speaking of customers who can't decide, one lady came in and read the list of our 4 soups from the menu. The soups were 4 soups that were nothing like Chicken Noodle, yet she asked us, "Which soup is the most like Chicken Noodle?" Ummmm...none of them.

An elderly woman, a "Regular" (as we call them) always asks for a CHOPPED salad. We're not sure what she means...her salad chopped as opposed to everything in one piece??! One-piece salads are not on the menu. This same woman wanted to try the soup because she was buying it for her husband, who wasn't present. But she didn't want to taste it herself, so she asked one of our employees to taste it for her! (Update: I recently found out that there is such a thing as a 'chopped salad.' However, I still don't know what it is).

Customer: "Do you know the tuna sandwich that someone made for me a couple weeks ago?"

Us: "No, I don't, but I can make you any sandwich that you want".

Customer: "But I don't know what was on it."

Us: "Neither do I."

One customer asked for a bottled water. "Small or large?" asked the Cashier. The man answered, "Oh, are there different sizes?" The cashier nodded. "Yes, we have small, large or seltzer." The man said, "I'll take a small." He paid and then walked over to the cooler. He looked at the bottles (all the same small size) in one of the coolers and called over to the cashier seriously, "Which ones are small and which ones are large???"

A customer asked for his sandwich on "wrapped bread." We don't know what that is. Apparently he couldn't decide whether to order a wrap or bread.

RESTAURANT ETIQUETTE

A middle-aged couple dressed in tennis clothes came in, and apparently couldn't keep their hands off each other. While waiting in line to order, the man put his hands down the lady's skirt. When they sat down to eat, she took off her shoes and put her foot in his...well, you get the idea.

***

A large man came in reeking of BODY ODOR. The other customers moved away. Two of them (father and son) actually SNIFFED each other to see if it was them. It wasn't.

Many customers with babies and young children plop them down on our counter where we put the customers' food. We know people think their kids are perfect, but we often find it necessary to ask them to remove their child's 'bacteria butt' or ask to kindly remove their diapered bottom from the counter where we serve food...only we say it nicer.

BEYOND RUDE

All the employees have their own opinions about which customers were the rudest. Here is one of mine...

A group of men came in and sat around for quite a while without ordering. They mentioned that they were waiting for someone. As it got closer to closing time, we reminded them that we were going to close in a little while and if they wanted to order they should do so. They ordered, sat down to eat, and eventually we put up the CLOSED sign. As we were putting it up, their friend came in and we kindly allowed him to order anyway. Then we proceeded to clean up and all the other customers left. Finally, they were the last group there, and even while we put up all the chairs around them, and they were finished eating, they continued to sit and talk, even while we were sweeping around them. In fact, while we were sweeping, they *KICKED SOME TRASH TOWARD US*. Ugh. Finally we were standing by the door in our coats saying goodbye, and they got up, leaving all their garbage all over their table instead of throwing it in the trash can. Ugh. Some people!

HORRIBLE BUT TRUE

Two girls and a baby were eating at the back table. After lunch, they lay their baby on the table, changed the diaper, and threw the dirty diaper in our trash. You never know what just transpired at your table in a restaurant!

MOST DISGUSTING CUSTOMER QUESTION

A very dirty-looking man came into the restaurant carrying a backpack...perhaps a hiker?? He meandered around a while, then finally came up to the counter. He held up a disgusting-looking dirty piece of cloth and asked if we could heat it up in our microwave. He said he was using it to help his back feel better. EWWWW. We don't even put customers' clean-looking *food* in our microwave. That dirty cloth had been inside his pants!! That would be akin to asking us if we could "please heat up these *underpants* in your microwave!!!"

BALD-FACED LIE

A woman came in and asked if we had any soups that weren't on the list. She said her 95 year old friend *only* liked Cream of Mushroom Soup. Our kind manager immediately said that she would make that soup the next day, and the woman said she would be back to get it. Well, the next day and several weeks went by and we never heard from the woman. Then one day she came back in again asking about "Soups that weren't on the Special Board." I recognized her and said, "Aren't you the lady who asked us to make that Cream of Mushroom soup for your friend?" and she turned red, shook her head vehemently and said "NO, That wasn't me!" I didn't say anything else about it, but I was tempted to say "I see your 95 year old friend in your car! Say hi for me." The lady ran out and quickly drove her friend away!

An "Assisted Living Bus" for elderly people stopped by our deli with a stream of slow-moving customers. As they came through the entrance door, we were horrified to see one elderly woman trip and fall down. Surrounded by her friends, we thought they would leap to her assistance. Instead, we could hear several of them muttering, "Get up, Agnes!! What the @*!&? is the matter with you?" as she struggled to her feet. Jeesh!!!

***

Sometimes the customers ask for items by economizing words. I assume they are actually asking, "Do you have any...?" rather than just shouting random words at us at high decibels.

Remember, most people who come in are starving for lunch, and that usually brings out their lower nature, not to mention their most confused selves. When they arrive at the cash register, some can barely speak when asked what kind of sandwiches they just ordered.

On the other hand, one customer who was standing at the counter under the "Order here" sign asked, "Should I order now?"

Us, silently: "Only if you're hungry."

CAT THERAPY:

A favorite customer (whom I know to be a therapist) ordered a ½ turkey & horseradish sandwich to share with her cat. I suggested (for the cat's sake) putting the horseradish on the side, but she said, "no, he will eat it." YOWZA!

KUSTOMERS with KIDS:

It's amazing to all of us how some adults will let their kids run rampant while they are ordering or eating...climbing all over the counters and décor, piling up all the ketchup and sugar packets, some even getting their heads stuck between panes of glass.

Equally annoying are those parents who are training their children in the art of decision making (something many of them could use a little of). Parents will hold up the line while they ask their toddlers whether they prefer hummus or avocado spread on their multigrain bread or whole wheat/white/marbled rye/honey oat/sub roll or 4 kinds of wrap)...and then which kind of our four cheeses, etc. Even many adult customers can barely make these decisions. Adults will often sigh, "Oh, so many decisions. Surprise me." Or worse, after they have chosen from the myriad of sandwiches on the menu, and are asked which bread they prefer, they groan, "ANOTHER decision to make!! UGH!!" To which we reply, "Well, I could make the sandwich the way I would like it!" at which point they might laugh sheepishly, but they are finally able to make a decision about their bread.

BELLRINGERS

A Bellringer is what we call a customer who is extremely rude and/or obnoxious. In fact, we have a bell sitting near the register, which we ring to let off some steam when we are treated badly. Nobody knows why we go directly from the customer to ring the bell, but WE all know why. In fact, usually all of us have just listened to the whole exchange.

Example: Here's the story of one arrogant, sarcastic, condescending customer, who stood by the register at the end of the day.

Manager: "Do you need something?"

Condescending Man: "No, I'm just standing here staring at all of you for no reason."

The Manager realizes he's being sarcastic (and condescending). She goes over to him and he says, "Your chicken sandwich was great, but your CHIPS...they were awful...blah blah blah..."

Manager, "I'm sorry, they sometimes turn out dark or light, depending on the potato, no one else complained, blah blah blah.."

Condescending Man: "So you're just gonna blow me off?!"

Manager: "No, I'm not blowing you off. What would you like me to do?"

Condescending Man: "I just told you I didn't like something...you need to make it right! Give me my money back."

Manager: "No, I'm not going to do that. There was nothing wrong with the chips."

Condescending Man: "Here's a piece of advice...when a customer doesn't like something, you need to make it right."

Manager: "There's nothing I can do. Nothing was wrong. No one else complained, people were happy with the chips all day."

Condescending Man: "Well, I will never be back!" (DING goes the bell)

Us (to ourselves): Is that a promise??

Moral: Chips are free. Chips are optional. We don't pay people NOT to get them. Or pay people if they get them and don't like them. If you don't like the chips, JUST...SAY...NO.

....

Condescending customers say things like, "GIVE ME a sandwich," or "I NEED a cup," instead of the obviously more polite, "May I please have a..." Another pet peeve is when a customer orders something, rattles off the description while we are still assembling the first 4 ingredients on the sandwich, and then nonchalantly goes on to order a few more sandwiches and throws out an insincere "please and thank-you" to save himself the bother of saying thank you after we are finished with the food.
(DING DING...see Bellringers, above)

Here's the story of a woman, who, while not an employee, was delivering something (gelato) to the Deli. She called and, without identifying herself as having a delivery for the Deli, said, "Where are you? I'm driving to (name of Deli)?"

Me: "Where are you coming from?"

Lady: "Rt. 7".

Me: "Are you coming north or south on 7?"

Lady: "I'm on Rt. 7."

Me: "Are you coming from (town north of us)?"

Lady: "I'm on 7. Which way do I go at exit 4?"

Me: "If you are coming south on Rt. 7, then you would turn right at Exit 4. We are on the right."

Lady: "There's (name of town east of us)"

Me: "Turn right on Exit 7."

Lady: "I see signs for (our town)."

Me: "See you when you get here." Click.

Lady: Ring! Ring! "We got disconnected. Where do I turn? Where's (name of Deli)? What does it look like?"

Me: "It's pink. I have to go now, I have customers."

Lady: "Where can I park my 16 wheeler?"

Me: "I have no idea. Not here."

Lady: "Well, what will I do? Where will I park it?"

Me: "I don't have any idea. I have to wait on some customers. See you later."

Shortly thereafter we saw a 16 wheeler in our driveway, knocking down tree branches as she backed in. (Uh-oh! I thought she was a customer with a 16 wheeler; it would have been helpful if she had mentioned that she had a delivery for us!)

UNBELIEVING CUSTOMERS

Customer: "I'd like a Turkey Club on toast."

Me: "We don't have a toaster."

Customer: "So you can't toast it then???"

Other Customer: (coming in the door when we are closed) "Is that closed sign real?" (No, it's just for fun).

COMPLAINERS

Is there anything customers won't complain about?? One woman called (actually took the time to CALL) to tell us she did not like the "trinkets" on our tables...um, those are salt and pepper shakers.

***

Recently after having lunch, a woman asked to speak to the manager. It seems she had a particular "beef." (a little deli humor there)...

She said, "I liked my lunch a lot, but I have a question for you. WHY ON EARTH don't you have stainless steel utensils instead of plastic ones? Surely a successful business like yours can afford to get a DISHWASHER?!" blah blah blah she went on and on. It's our deli, we can do what we want. So there.

BOB NEWHART

There was a customer who resembled the actor Bob Newhart. I asked him if he was Bob Newhart, and he said yes. I was SO excited! I asked him for his autograph for my dad, and he gave it to me. After he signed, I found out that he was NOT Bob Newhart, rather he thought it was funny that I thought he was. I was disappointed, embarrassed, and thought that was NOT funny. But oh well. But what was even less funny was a later time when he came in, ordered 2 sodas, one in a cup and one in a bottle. I asked him if he was sure he wanted both and he said yes. After he paid and took both the bottle and the cup, he sat down and had lunch. When he finished, he came back and was quite angry that I had charged him for both sodas. I said, "That's why I asked if you wanted both." He began yelling at the top of his lungs (I assume it was the top) "I'M RIGHT AND YOU'RE WRONG!!!!" while other customers looked on and shook their heads. I refused to back down this time, or to ever wait on this rude customer again. The real Bob Newhart would have never acted like that.

***

Different Strokes

The stories about our customers are endless. It took me only a little while to realize that while there are many different individuals in this world, as a whole there are 8 general categories that most customers fit into: SLOW: (People who have all day and want to make JUST the right decision about lunch); BEWILDERED (Never been in before, can't find the menu or cash register, can't read the many signs and don't know where anything is or are too confused to figure out the protocol and direction of the line flow and where the tables are, and who to give their order to); UNDECIDED (Don't know what they want to eat, think there are too many choices, would like someone else to choose their bread, soup or possibly their entire lunch); PLEASANT: (Obviously our favorites); IN A HURRY: (usually locals on a lunch break); TOO QUIET TO BE HEARD: (This is annoying. Usually mumblers are people who aren't sure of the correct ordering terminology;) or ON THEIR PHONE WHILE ORDERING: (a more and more common occurrence); IMPATIENT: Gruff and Rude (Self-explanatory and understandably our least favorite type of customer). I also would include here the people who order everything at once and expect us to remember everything they are saying while simultaneously making several sandwiches. For example: "Givemeaturkeysandwichwithlettuceandmayoandcheeseanda

roastbeefsubwiththeworksandmydaughterwouldlikeapeanutb
utterandjellynotmuchpeanutbutterandnopickleanddothesand
wichescomewithchips..." (pause for breath)...

Me: "What kind of bread for the first one?"

***

WHEN IT COMES DOWN TO IT, MANY PEOPLE ARE JUST
PLAIN RUDE, END OF STORY! But wait...

We generally understand that many people are impatient
out of feelings of imminent starvation, we get that, but
people, get a grip! When they veer off into sheer rudeness,
let's just say they do NOT get the best of anything. So here's
a word of advice: Don't be impatient, gruff or rude to
people in the food industry. They are people too. And
furthermore, to quote one of our employees, remember that
we are deli workers, not brain surgeons. If we forget to
leave out that pickle...give...us...a...break!

***

Speaking of Mumblers, we have noticed that unfortunately,
there are a certain group of people, invariably women (I call
them the Whisperers) who are apparently unable to order

lunch for themselves. When we ask them what they would like, they turn to the man they are with, whisper to him and then HE proceeds to order for both of them. These women refuse to meet our eyes, and sometimes they leave the line and sit down, leaving the man to pay and carry the food. Don't quite get it...how can there be so many women who can't speak out loud??

***

Customer at register, pointing to basket of food: "Is that our food?"

Me: "Have you ordered yet?"

Customer: "No."

Me: "Then it couldn't possibly be your food!" Bahahahahaha

"NO PICKLE!!!!"

Almost top of the list of familiar customer quotes, is the fearful shout of "NO PICKLE!!!!!!!" while we are wrapping their sandwiches to take-out. I must admit that although we get 99 percent of the orders right, to exclude a pickle when wrapping a sandwich is a hard habit for us to break.

We try our best, but sometimes, while watching us wrap the sandwich, it goes a little like this (with rising panic in their voices):

"No pickle! NO. PICKLE. NO

PICKLE!!!!!!!!!!!!!!!!!!!!!!!!!!!!!!!!!!!!!!

ALLERGIES

While some people appear to be deathly afraid of the dreaded pickle, other customers are "worried" about other foods, such as green peppers or whether the chips are crispy or not.

Then there are the customers who want to know if there is gluten in our salad dressing, or the hummus, or anything. People, most of you are NOT allergic to gluten. I know it's the latest fad, and sounds 'cool' to be allergic/avoiding gluten, but statistics show only a VERY small percentage of people are truly allergic to gluten. So, unless you have been tested and know YOU are one of those people, there is no reason to hold up the line for 20 minutes asking about every one of our foods and dressings and whether it has gluten in it. First of all, we don't know what is in every food and dressing we buy. We don't even know all the foods that have gluten in them. So if you are TRULY allergic, educate yourself about what it is in every food you might encounter. And if in doubt, just order a salad! Even I know salads have no gluten.

NUT ALLERGIES are a little different. If a person has a nut allergy, or a child with a nut allergy, they shouldn't be taking a chance eating out in the first place...especially when a restaurant tells you that they have nuts everywhere! We can do our best (such as changing our gloves for you, trying to avoid peanut butter, walnuts, etc.) but in the end it is the customer's responsibility to avoid places that tell you they are NOT nut free. To eat there with a nut allergy is just plain...well, you know...!

***

Alright, some people are annoying and but there are others who are actually certifiable. One such customer was in the Deli recently. In the middle of a lunch rush, everything was running smoothly as usual...until we heard a piercing screech and a woman's voice shouting VERY loudly: "She grabbed my arm! She grabbed my arm! She touched me. Call the police! She's not supposed to touch me...she grabbed my ARM.!!!!" At first no one knew what was going on. There was a woman going down the steps shouting and looking back at a sweet older woman who was sitting quietly with her husband. Someone (thankfully) guided the paranoid woman out of the restaurant and then we heard that during lunch, the yelling woman had already been rude to the sitting woman by insisting to everyone around her that "SHE"S LOOKING AT ME!" and "STOP STARING AT MEEEEEEEEEE!" Hoo-boy

Which reminds me of the woman who got enraged when one of our employees was SMILING. In an extreme case of paranoia she accused the young girl of smiling for sinister reasons and said that her smile was "upsetting her friend" who was sitting up in the dining room not even looking at the smiling employee.

MENU MISPRONUNCIATIONS:

(I will include here customers that cannot identify exactly what they would like for lunch)

Customer: "Hoo-moose"   (Hummus)

"Bone-Yard" (I presume they meant a Barnyard")

"Back-yard" instead of a "Barnyard." (What's next..a Front-Yard?")

"I ordered a "Veggie-Wedgie" (Why are you throwing in the word Wedgie?? The sandwich is simply called a Veggie)

Question: What happens to peoples' brains between looking at the menu to turning their heads and speaking to us???

"Turkey Rockel" or "Turkey Roshel" (Turkey Rachel)

This is a common mistake: "I will have a Pastrami River"
(No, you won't, it's called a Pastrami ROver)

"Kye-oat" (Coyote)

"Turkey Supreme" or "Turkey Royalist" (Turkey Royal)

"The Rainbow" (The Ranger)

"Butter Squash" (Butternut Squash) This was written on the menu board by one of our own. We make mistakes, too!

"Nature's Way" (The Nature Wrap..since when did it become an address?)

"Roast Beef, please, with horsey-mayo" (A little baby talk for Horseradish perhaps???)

"Buffalo Joe" (Who's that? It's a Buffalo BILL)

"The Natural" (It's not a movie title, it's called a NATURE WRAP)

"I'll have a Rachel Rover" (Make up your mind...those are 2 different sandwiches)

"Marbelized Rye" (Really?? It's MARBLED Rye, not marbleized!

Our Deli name is the name of a girl, so we have many customers who point at me and ask, "Are you __ (name of Restaurant)?" Me, pointing to huge dog head in tile in front of me, "No, this is__'"

***

Customer, "I'll have turkey on toasted sourdough with a little mozzarella." Um...no you won't. We don't have that. Neither will you have avocado, liverwurst, or brie...or bologna, pumpernickel or baguettes. Or breakfast, for that matter. And no, we do not have any muffins, eggs, or bagels. Seriously, we don't have things that aren't on the menu.

We have a ½ Sandwich & Soup Special. Many many customers order this and proceed to tell us what kind of ½ soup they would like. They also try to order a ½ SALAD ½ soup but that doesn't exist, either.

***

Me, to customer ordering a sandwich: "What kind of bread would you like that on?" Customer, pointing seriously to giant cookie. "That kind."

Customer, ordering a sandwich that comes with horseradish: "Is that horseradish hot?"

Me: "Well, it's horseradish…"

***

There is one customer who is particularly hard to understand what he is trying to order. It is bad enough that he mumbles, but he gets angry when we don't understand what he is saying. He obviously can talk understandably most of the time, because you can get a majority of the sentence. For example, he will say, "Can I get a ham sandwich with (mumble mumble)." To which we reply, "Anything on that?" And he will respond, "Yeah, chatt-uh."

Us: "Excuse me?" Him: "CHATT-UH!!" (If you didn't understand it either, he was asking for cheddar. I only know that because once his sister reluctantly translated for him).

HEARD IT BEFORE:

Here are some statements from customers that we have heard many, many, times, although each (I'm sure) thinks they are the first ones to say this:

Holding a cookie up to their friend: "These are as big as your head." And "That's not a cookie, it's a pizza." "This is as big as a plate." "Do you have any bigger cookies?" And so on.

The cookies are on the counter in front of us, with signs in front of each kind of cookie. The signs are pointing toward the customer, naturally, not at us. Invariably, a customer will say something like, "Don't you have any chocolate chip cookies?!?"

Us: "Let's see, that looks like a chocolate chip. But there are signs in front of each cookie, and I can't see them."

Customer: "Oh! They are all mixed up!!" (as if WE mixed them up, not the customers that have been standing there touching them all day).

***

Us, to customer: "Would you like chips?"

The two standard answers are: "Does anyone ever say no?!" (yes) or "That's the reason I come here!"

***

A typical customer exchange: "Can you grill this sandwich?"

Us: "No, sorry. We don't have a grill."

Customer: "But you have a frying pan right there!"

Us (In our Minds) "That is not how we operate. If we wanted to fry each sandwich you would be here all day."

About the toaster...we don't have one. Customers: "I'll have a BLT on toasted white." Us: "Sorry, we don't have a toaster." Most customers: "Ohhhhhh. Ok." Some say ok. Others go completely back to the menu. Others go on a rampage.

HAMMING IT UP BEHIND THE SCENES

All of us at the deli love laughing, at ourselves, each other,
and umm, some of the more humorous incidents that have
occurred at our deli. That is the main reason why this book
was written; so we never forget how hilarious deli life can
be. We can find humor and make a story about almost
anything, from a vegetable with a strange shape to the rude

way a customer slammed the door when they found out we were closed. Humor is how we deal with the stresses inherent in a fast-paced business, and humor is the way we enjoy and remember experiences with others who completely understand and share our deli life.

Often at work, we reminisce about all the funny things that have happened. Some things are what customers said and did, but there are also funny things we have said and done, mistakes we have made, and names we have for some of our most memorable customers. (We don't know their names, so when referring to them, we have to call them SOMETHING). Here are some of the names that come to mind: "Iced Tea Thieves," "Bushy Brows", "Gelato Woman," "Bob Newhart," "FBI Man," "Kielbasa and Cabbage Woman" and others. We remember all of the incidents that have happened, good and bad, but mostly the funny ones. We remember the time I went up to wait on someone and as soon as I said, "Can I help you?" I suddenly remembered something else I had to do and walked away, leaving the customer standing there, speechless. We remember the time another employee was standing at the register while a customer gushed, "Your deli is so amazing. It's the best deli I have ever been to," while the employee just stared past them blankly like a frozen statue and didn't respond. We also remember the time when one of us made a turkey sandwich and forgot to put the turkey on it, and a million times when someone said "NO PICKLE!" and we put it in anyway, out of habit.

PROVO-LEAVE US-ALONE

(We Close at 2)

We have short hours at the Deli. Most days we are open only 10:30 a.m. to 2:00 p.m. However, we arrive between 7 and 8 a.m. and leave around 2:30.

At precisely 2:00 p.m. we put up our closed signs. Many customers will ignore our signs and try to get served. We can't lock the doors because we still have customers finishing their lunches in the dining room and they will need to get out.

Here are some comments from some of our most memorable latecomers when it is AFTER closing time:

"Can't you just make me a sandwich?!?" (no, we are closed)

"I'm starving!!!" (I'm sorry, we're closed)

"I came all the way from New Jersey (that's about 500 miles) just for the chips!!!" (I'm sorry, they are gone and we are closed)

"Is that 'closed sign' real???" (Yes)

My favorite: "Don't you have anything just lying around?" (Yes, the garbage and some crumbs)

Me, to a customer trying to order a sandwich after closing time. "We're out of bread!"

Customer looks at the piles of bread still sitting there. Brow furrows doubtfully.

Me: "Well, we're closed!"

Customer: "What time do you *close* close?" (HUH?!?!).

Us: "Well we close at 2, but we *close close* at 2..."

Sometimes when people come in a couple minutes before closing time, we warn them that we are about to close, in case they wanted to linger over lunch.

"Ma'am, just wanted to let you know we are closing in 2 minutes."

Lady: No response.

Two minutes later she hasn't ordered, so another employee ventures: "Ma'am, we are closing, would you like to order now?"

Lady: "I KNOW you're closing...they told me FOUR TIMES that you are closing!!" Sheesh...such anger.

***

Some customers try to sneak in after the closed sign is up. One enterprising woman came up to the window and we saw her looking at the three closed signs, then she went to her car and *called* us trying to place an order. "I know it says you're closed, but....."

When 3 or 4 'closed' signs don't convey the message that we are closed, we have a few tricks up our sleeves for getting people to leave: Putting the vacant chairs up on the tables. Wiping the tables around them. Sweeping around the customers. Turning the music up louder. Turning the music OFF. And my personal favorite, saying goodbye loudly to each other.

Eventually we are all finished cleaning up and waiting by the door. Customers: "Oh, I didn't know you were closing!"

VALUABLE ADVICE

As most everyone is a patron at a deli at one time or another, and as someone on the "other side of the counter", allow me to give you some very valuable advice...

1 Don't anger or annoy anyone who is preparing or serving your food!

2 Don't order something and then wander away. Your server has important questions to ask you, such as what kind of bread do you want, is that for here or to go?? If you leave your server hanging, your order may just get left on the counter waiting for the next step while the server moves on to the customer who IS staying at the counter to order.

3 Don't tell the server all the sandwiches you are ordering at once. Be considerate, and order them one at a time. "We are deli workers, not brain surgeons." (Quote by a brilliant co-worker I will call "L")

4 Unless you are REALLY unable to, please read the menu and the signs. We are trying to help many people and it slows things down for everyone if we have to list all the items that are actually listed in plain sight.

5 Don't be talking on your cell phone while trying to place an order. We will ignore you and go on to the polite customer behind you.

6 Don't "shush" us by holding up one finger as a signal to us that you're not ready to order. That is the height of

rudeness. I can't be responsible for what will happen to your food. Just kidding...or am I??????

7 Don't wave at me to get my attention, ESPECIALLY if I'm already looking at you!!!

8 Don't ask me to break a hundred dollar bill when your total purchase is $1.63 and don't ask me to break a hundred when you are one of the first customers of the day. EVERYONE has a credit card; this is the time to use it.

9 Don't argue over who is paying the bill and then involve the casher by asking us "not" to take your friend's money. We want no part of your little game. We really don't have time or care who pays.

10 Don't try to hand the cashier your garbage.

11 Finally, and maybe most important, believe it when you see a CLOSED sign on the door. Yes, it is real. Yes, we are finished making food, and now we are cleaning up. Don't ask us to make "just one sandwich", tell us how far you drove to get there, argue about what time you think it really is, or ask to use the bathroom. CLOSED means NOT OPEN...for any reason.

As time goes on, and I have worked in the deli for the past 9 years, I find myself a little more jaded about customers, but not people in general. There are still enough good, kind people (some of whom are even customers) who smile, ask us how our day is going, and order politely. They even return lost wallets and keys with honesty, and some admit when they break or spill a bottle of juice. Not everyone barks at us rudely, and not everyone orders us around like peons; some will even stop to chat and laugh with us, compliment the food, and tell us how quickly we made their lunch, which keeps us from biting the heads off of all of the rude customers. When we ask, "Can I help you?" you just never know what is going to come out of their mouths. Therefore, we take all of their guff like the professionals that we are, with a smile (mostly) and with a professional demeanor which shows we are mature and invested in the customer service business. Why? Because we have to...we are Deli Workers.

Printed in Great Britain
by Amazon.co.uk, Ltd.,
Marston Gate.